3

GROOKS

GROOKS

Piet Hein

with the assistance of
Jens Arup

THE M.I.T. PRESS
Massachusetts Institute of Technology
Cambridge, Massachusetts, and London, England

ARS BREVIS

There is
one art,
no more,
no less:
to do
all things
with art-
lessness.

PROBLEMS

Problems worthy
of attack
prove their worth
by hitting back.

THE ETERNAL TWINS

Taking fun
 as simply fun
and earnestness
 in earnest
shows how thoroughly
 thou none
of the two
 discernest.

CONSOLATION GROOK

Losing one glove
is certainly painful,
but nothing
    compared to the pain
of losing one,
throwing away the other,
and finding
    the first one again.

T. T. T.

Put up in a place
where it's easy to see
the cryptic admonishment
    T. T. T.

When you feel how depressingly
slowly you climb,
it's well to remember that
    Things Take Time.

OMNISCIENCE

Knowing what
thou knowest not
is in a sense
omniscience.

SIMPLY ASSISTING GOD

I am a humble artist
molding my earthly clod,
adding my labor to nature's,
simply assisting God.

Not that my effort is needed;
yet somehow, I understand,
my maker has willed it that I too should have
unmolded clay in my hand.

HINT AND SUGGESTION

Admonitory grook addressed to youth

The human spirit sublimates
the impulses it thwarts;
a healthy sex life mitigates
the lust for other sports.

MANKIND

Men, said the Devil,
are good to their brothers:
they don't want to mend
their own ways but each other's.

NAÏVE

Naïve you are
if you believe
life favors those
who aren't naïve.

THE MIRACLE OF SPRING

We glibly talk
    of nature's laws,
but do things have
    a natural cause?

Black earth becoming
    yellow crocus
is undiluted
    hocus-pocus.

DREAM INTERPRETATION
Simplified

Everything's either
concave or -vex,
so whatever you dream
will be something with sex.

PRAYER
to the sun above the clouds

Sun that givest all things birth,
shine on everything on earth!

If that's too much to demand,
shine at least on this our land.

If even that's too much for thee,
shine at any rate on me.

CIRCUMSCRIPTURE
or The Holy Navigator

As Pastor X steps out of bed,
    he slips a neat disguise on:
that halo round his priestly head
    is really his horizon.

SOCIAL MECHANISM

When people always
try to take
the very smallest
piece of cake,
how can it also
always be
that that's the one
that's left for me?

A TOAST

The soul may be a mere pretense,
the mind makes very little sense.
So let us value the appeal
of that which we can taste and feel.

ON PROBLEMS

Our choicest plans
   have fallen through,
our airiest castles
   tumbled over,
because of lines
   we neatly drew
and later neatly
   stumbled over.

AN ETHICAL GROOK

I see
    and I hear
        and I speak no evil;
I carry
    no malice
        within my breast;
yet quite without
    wishing
        a man to the Devil
one may be
    permitted
        to hope for the best.

LILAC TIME

The lilacs are flowering, sweet and sublime
   with a perfume that goes to the head;
and lovers meander, in prose and rhyme,
trying to say—
      for the thousandth time—
   what's easier done than said.

THE DOUBLE-DOOR EFFECT

Double-doors are justified
because they're comfortably wide.
Therefore you only half undo'em;
and therefore nothing can get through'em.

FORETASTE WITH AFTERTASTE

Corinna's scanty evening dress
reveals her charms to an excess
which makes a fellow lust for less.

MAJORITY RULE

His party was the Brotherhood of Brothers,
and there were more of them than of the others.
That is, they constituted that minority
which formed the greater part of the majority.
Within the party, he was of the faction
that was supported by the greater fraction.
And in each group, within each group, he sought
the group that could command the most support.
The final group had finally elected
a triumvirate whom they all respected.
Now of these three, two had the final word,
because the two could overrule the third.
One of these two was relatively weak,
so one alone stood at the final peak.
He was THE GREATER NUMBER of the pair
which formed the most part of the three that were
elected by the most of those whose boast
it was to represent the most of most
of most of most of the entire state—
or of the most of it at any rate.
He never gave himself a moment's slumber
but sought the welfare of the greatest number.
And all the people, everywhere they went,
knew to their cost exactly what it meant
to be dictated to by the majority.
But that meant nothing—they were the minority.

EXPERTS

Experts have
their expert fun
ex cathedra
telling one
just how nothing
can be done.

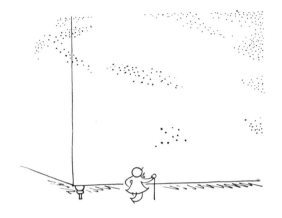

ATOMYRIADES

Nature, it seems, is the popular name
for milliards and milliards and milliards
of particles playing their infinite game
of billiards and billiards and billiards.

ROAD SENSE
The paradox of rationalization

God save us, now they're murdering
    another winding road,
and another lovely countryside
    will take another load
    of pantechnicon and car and motorbike.
They're busy making bigger roads,
    and better roads and more,
so that people can discover
    even faster than before
    that everything is everywhere alike.

OUR NOBLEST ACHIEVEMENT

We must expect posterity
to view with some asperity
the marvels and the wonders
we're passing on to it;
but it should change its attitude
to one of heartfelt gratitude
when thinking of the blunders
we didn't quite commit.

THE TRUE DEFENSE

The only defense
that is more than pretense
is to act on the fact
that there is no defense.

PAST PLUPERFECT

The past—well, it's just like
    our dear Great-Aunt Laura,
who cannot or will not perceive
that though she is welcome,
    and though we adore her
yet now it is time to leave.

MY FAITH IN DOCTORS

My faith in doctors
        is immense.
Just one thing spoils it:
        their pretense
of authorized
        omniscience.

DEFENSE WANTED

In International
   Consequences
the players must reckon
   to reap what they've sown.
We have a defense
   against other defenses,
But what's to defend us
   against our own?

GETTING DOWN TO FUNDAMENTALS

It will steadily shrink,
our earthly abode,
until antipode stands
upon antipode.

Then, soles together,
the planet gone,
we'll know the ground
that we rest upon.

GROOK TO STIMULATE GRATITUDE

in sour rationalists

As things so
　　very often are
intelligence
　　won't get you far.

So be glad
　　you've got more sense
than you've got
　　intelligence.

MISSING LINK

Man's a kind
of Missing Link,
fondly thinking
he can think.

THE ROAD TO WISDOM

The road to wisdom? —Well, it's plain
and simple to express:
        Err
        and err
        and err again
        but less
        and less
        and less.

THAT IS THE QUESTION
Hamlet anno Domini

Coexistence
or no existence.

BRIDGE OR TUNNEL?
Channel project

A tunnel would be possible,
  a bridge would also do,
but wouldn't it be better to
  amalgamate the two?

Let bridge and tunnel undulate
  in waves from shore to shore,
keeping green the memories
  of those who went before.

LOSING   FACE

The noble art of losing face
may one day save the human race
and turn into eternal merit
what weaker minds would call disgrace.

A PSYCHOLOGICAL TIP

Whenever you're called on to make up your mind,
    and you're hampered by not having any,
the best way to solve the dilemma, you'll find,
    is simply by spinning a penny.

No—not so that chance shall decide the affair
    while you're passively standing there moping;
but the moment the penny is up in the air,
    you suddenly know what you're hoping.

MORE HASTE

Inscription for a monument
at the crossroads

Here lies, extinguished in his prime,
a victim of modernity:
but yesterday he hadn't time—
and now he has eternity.

A WORD TO THE WISE

Let the world pass in its time-ridden race;
    never get caught in its snare.
Remember, the only acceptable case
for being in any particular place
    is having no business there.

MEETING THE EYE

You'll probably find
that it suits your book
to be a bit cleverer
than you look.

Observe that the easiest
method by far
is to look a bit stupider
than you are.

IF YOU KNOW WHAT I MEAN

A poet should be of the
   old-fashioned meaningless brand:
obscure, esoteric, symbolic—
   the critics demand it;
so if there's a poem of mine
   that you do understand
I'll gladly explain what it means
   till you don't understand it.

THE CASE FOR OBSCURITY

On thoughts and words

If no thought
your mind does visit,
make your speech
not too explicit.

LEST FOOLS SHOULD FAIL

True wisdom knows
it must comprise
some nonsense
as a compromise,
lest fools should fail
to find it wise.

GROOK ON LONG-WINDED AUTHORS

Long-winded writers I abhor,
 and glib, prolific chatters;
give me the ones who tear and gnaw
 their hair and pens to tatters:
who find their writing such a chore
 they only write what matters.

OUT OF TIME

A holiday thought

My old clock used to tell the time
    and subdivide diurnity;
but now it's lost both hands and chime
    and only tells eternity.

AN ODE TO MODESTY

Talking of successful rackets
modesty deserves a mention.
Exclamation marks in brackets
never fail to draw attention.

THE CURE FOR EXHAUSTION

Sometimes, exhausted
with toil and endeavor,
I wish I could sleep
for ever and ever;
but then this reflection
my longing allays:
I shall be doing it
one of these days.

I'D LIKE—

I'd like to know
what this whole show
is all about
before it's out.

A MAXIM FOR VIKINGS

Here is a fact
　　that should help you fight
　　　a bit longer:

Things that don't act-
　　ually kill you outright
　　　make you stronger.

MAKING   SENSE

Life makes sense,
and who could doubt it,
if we have
no doubt
no doubt about it.

A MOMENT'S THOUGHT

As eternity
is reckoned,
there's a lifetime
in a second.

LIVING   IS—

Living is
    a thing you do
now or never—
    which do you?

INDEX OF TITLES

INDEX OF FIRST LINES